My Child Won't Sleep

Also by Sujay Kansagra, MD

Everything I Learned in Medical School: Besides All the Book Stuff

MY CHILD WON'T SLEEP: A Quick Guide for the Sleep-Deprived Parent

Sujay M. Kansagra, MD
Director, Duke Pediatric Neurology
Sleep Medicine Program

ISBN-13: 978-1499340921
ISBN-10: 1499340923

For the sleep-deprived, young and old.

Contents

Preface

Sleep is a beautiful thing. Yet a process as natural as sleep is the source of constant frustration for so many. This frustration is magnified when it is a child with sleep difficulties. Along with the exhaustion and fatigue comes endless advice from friends and family who think they are the expert, based on their own personal experience. A simple Internet search for solutions adds feelings of despair and perhaps guilt, given the variety of strong opinions and emotions that surround the subject. *Do I let them cry? Do I let them grow out of it? Is it a medical problem? Am I doing something wrong?* You likely have many questions.

Here is the reality: *the solutions for most cases of childhood "insomnia" are not complicated and can be learned in less than the time a child needs for a nap.* But no single solution works for every child and family. So my goal is to present the effective options and let you decide which method fits you and your child best. The solutions presented in this book apply to otherwise healthy children. If your child has any medical or psychiatric conditions, please talk with your doctor before using these techniques.

For the latest information on sleep and sleep disorders, follow me on Twitter (@PedsSleepDoc).

Let's get started.

~ Chapter 1 ~
The Basics: What Every Child Needs

No discussion about sleep should begin without first talking about the foundation for sleep—good sleep hygiene. Sleep hygiene is a combination of our behaviors and the things around us that can help or hurt our sleep. There are four basic elements of good sleep hygiene.

Sleep Routine

Everyone should have a sleep routine—adults included. A sleep routine is a set of activities that are performed the same way and begin at the same time every night leading to bedtime. These activities should help your child wind down. For infants, the routine can include feeding your child, changing his or her diaper/clothes, reading him or her a story, etc. For older children, it can include taking a shower, brushing teeth, changing into pajamas, and reading. The goal is to have quiet activities that avoid too much light exposure and mental stimulation. A good routine should be about twenty to thirty minutes in length.

Appropriate Sleep Schedule

How many hours of sleep does a child need? How many naps should a child take? The answers vary from child to child and change as children grow. Here is a rough guideline based on age. The "Average Sleep Needed" column is based on total sleep in a twenty-four-hour time period (naps included).

Age	Average Sleep Needed	# of Naps
0–3 Months	12–18 hours	3+
3–12 Months	14–15 hours	2-4
1–3 years	12–14 hours	1-2
3–5 years	11–13 hours	0-1
5–10 years	10–12 hours	None
10–17 years	8.5–10 hours	None
Adults	7–9 hours	None

The take-away message is that the duration of normal sleep is a range, and every child is different. A minority of people do not fit even within the ranges provided above.

A Comfortable Environment

This is obvious, but the environment should be a comfortable temperature and free from excessive noise.

Body temperature drops during sleep, and being too warm can inhibit the ability to fall asleep. Therefore, I typically recommend keeping the room on the slightly cooler side and dressing warmly instead of the opposite.

Avoidance and Treatment of Sleep Disruptors

One major sleep disruptor is caffeine. Even morning caffeine in the form of coffee, tea, soda, or chocolate can disrupt nighttime sleep. As a rule, I recommend that children not consume any substances with caffeine, regardless of whether or not there is a sleep issue.

Medical problems can also disrupt sleep, including nasal congestion from allergies, eczema, and gastroesophageal reflux (heartburn). These should be treated by your pediatrician.

Once you have the basic foundation of good sleep hygiene in place, you are ready to move on.

~ Chapter 2 ~

My Infant Won't Sleep: Ages 6 months–1 year

The most common problem at this age is the inability to sleep through the night. If there is one incredibly important point I can make, it's this: *no child sleeps through the night*. In fact, no human being sleeps through the night. We all have multiple awakenings while we sleep—most commonly after we complete a sleep cycle. For infants, a sleep cycle is about fifty to sixty minutes; for older children and adults, it's ninety minutes. During a sleep cycle, you dip into deeper stages of sleep and then come back out into lighter sleep. Here is a graph of how a night's sleep might look. This is simplified, but it should help you understand sleep cycles and the fact that no one sleeps through the night.

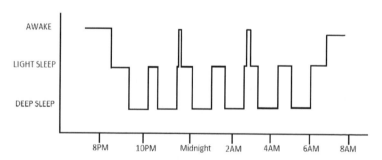

So, if *all* children wake up at night, why does your child start screaming and others don't? It's because some children can't go back to sleep on their own. Why can't some children go back to sleep? At this age, the answer is usually sleep onset associations.

What are Sleep Onset Associations?

Sleep onset associations are essentially anything in our environment that we associate with falling asleep. For example, an adult who says, "I need the TV on to go to sleep" has developed a sleep association. No one really needs a TV to fall asleep. But someone who always falls asleep with the TV on will eventually feel that he or she "needs" it to fall asleep. This individual has associated the transition from wake to sleep with the television and therefore feels the need to have the television on during bedtime. It can become difficult for such an adult to fall asleep without the television.

We start to develop sleep associations very early in life. By six months of age, children are very perceptive and aware of their environment when they go to sleep. Sleep onset associations can form in children when an intervention

5

from a caregiver is used to help a child fall asleep. The child learns that this intervention is always present during the transition from wake to sleep. Some examples of these interventions include: rocking the child, singing to the child, holding the child, playing music, feeding the child, sleeping next to the child, and driving the child around in a car. The child learns to transition from wake to sleep with the help of these interventions. Then, when the child wakes up *during a normal awakening (which, remember, all children have as a normal part of their sleep cycle),* the child expects the same intervention to be present to help return to sleep.

If it is not present, the child will cry until the intervention is put in place. The child has not learned how to fall asleep without this intervention. This is popularly known as the inability to "self-soothe." This is why some children wake up and cry repeatedly through the night. And the crying tends to occur after a full sleep cycle, which can be as often as every sixty to ninety minutes, with one to five awakenings each night. Does this sound familiar?

So, when a child has a completely normal awakening during the night, it will result in one of two scenarios:

1. The child cries because he or she needs a caregiver intervention (the association) to go back

6

to sleep, so parents have to perform the same "trick" they used to put him or her to sleep initially, such as feeding or rocking.

2. Or, the child looks around briefly and goes back to sleep, and the parents happily report that their child is "sleeping through the night."

The Solution

How do we go from the first scenario to the second scenario? First, we have to identify the sleep associations for the child (hint: there can be more than one) and secondly, teach the child to transition to sleep without these associations. This is commonly known as "sleep training." There are a variety of ways to approach sleep training, and it really depends on what you as the caregiver are comfortable doing. No matter what anyone tells you, there is no "right" way to sleep train your child.

Since every parenting style and every child is different, the key is picking the solution that you can stick to. The two most important aspects to picking a solution are: determining how comfortable you are with crying and how quickly you want the problem solved. Some caretakers cannot tolerate an infant crying for more than five seconds, while others can withstand hours of crying if they feel it is best for the child. Similarly, for some families the problem has become so bad that a change is needed immediately, whereas others are comfortable with a slow, gradual approach. The solutions presented vary in amount of crying and typical response time. Again, there is no right and wrong. You must choose what you can stick with because, at the end of the day, you will be the main determinant of whether sleep training succeeds.

Let's go over the options. Each of these techniques has the same goal, which is *ensuring that the child starts going to sleep without caregiver interventions.* Pick which solution you feel works best for you and your child. It is important to not feel guilty, no matter which method you use. Sleep training is not for the parent's benefit, it is for the child's benefit (more on this later). Please remember that these methods are for healthy children without any other medical or psychiatric conditions. Please discuss the techniques with your doctor before attempting to sleep train if you have any concerns regarding the health of your child.

Solution 1: The Cold-Turkey Method

Type of caregiver: Can withstand a large amount of crying.
Typical length of training: A few days.
Other common names for this method: Extinction, Cry-it-Out.

Step 1: Determine what time the child is currently falling asleep on a typical night. This is the new bedtime. Note: this should not be the time you are placing the child in bed, but the time he or she actually falls asleep.

Step 2: Develop a consistent nighttime routine that starts twenty to thirty minutes prior to this new bedtime and is performed the same way each night. This can include anything you and your child find relaxing, such as nursing, singing, bathing, etc. *The child should still be awake after the routine.*

Step 3: Place child into crib/bed after the routine, *while he or she is still awake.* This should be around the time that the child is currently falling asleep on a typical night.

Step 4: Leave. Do not return, regardless of how long the child cries.

If the child wakes up in the middle of the night: Do nothing.

While these steps sound simple, the process can be difficult. Children with sleep onset associations can cry for hours—yes, hours! They are angry that they are not getting what they want, and they will let you know about it. The reason this technique fails so often is that caregivers eventually give in. But the nice thing about sleep is that at some point, everyone *must* go to sleep. There is no avoiding it. In order for this technique to work, you must refuse to give in to the crying, regardless of how long it lasts.

If you take the cold-turkey approach, I recommend using a video monitor (with the volume turned down) that will allow you to periodically check to ensure that your child is safe while still avoiding interaction with the child. Alternatively, you can remain in the room with the child as long as you can completely ignore the crying and not interact in any way. If you can withstand the crying, this is a fast way to sleep train your child. Be aware that the second and third nights are often even harder than the first, but it should improve after this. You just have to make it through the first few difficult nights.

Once the child learns to fall asleep without your intervention, you can slowly move the routine and bedtime earlier by ten or fifteen minutes each night until reaching the desired bedtime.

Solution 2: The Wait-and-Check Method

Type of caregiver: Can tolerate a moderate amount of crying.
Typical length of training: Less than one week.
Other common names for this method: Graduated Extinction, Ferber Method, Controlled Crying, Controlled Comforting.

Step 1: Determine what time the child is currently falling asleep on a typical night. This is the new bedtime. Note: this should not be the time you are placing the child in bed, but the time he or she actually falls asleep.

Step 2: Develop a consistent nighttime routine that starts twenty to thirty minutes prior to this new bedtime and is performed the same way each night. This can include anything you and your child find relaxing, such as nursing, singing, bathing, etc. *The child should still be awake after the routine.*

Step 3: Place child into crib/bed after the routine while he or she is still awake. This should be around the time the child typically falls asleep.

Step 4: Leave.

Step 5: On the first night, wait for five minutes of crying, then go back into the room and try to soothe your child briefly (up to one minute maximum). Do not pick up the child. Simply pat the child and say something reassuring. Then leave, even if the child is not completely soothed. Wait ten minutes before checking in again, soothe the child briefly, and then leave. Then wait fifteen minutes and repeat the process. Extend your check-in time by five minutes with each check until your child is asleep. Only go into the room if your child is actively crying. Your child *must* fall asleep while you are out of the room.

Step 6: On the second night, start your first check at ten minutes and add five minutes for each subsequent check that night. On the third night, start the first check at fifteen minutes. Add an additional five minutes each subsequent night.

If the child wakes up in the middle of the night: Repeat the same process, starting your check-in at the same time you did at the beginning of the night. Go into the room only if your child is awake and actively crying. Remember that children make many different noises in their sleep.

This is perhaps the most well-known form of sleep training. Popularized by Dr. Richard Ferber, it is well suited for the parent who is determined to sleep train and who can withstand a moderate amount of crying. Feel free to make your own plan for the number of minutes prior to checking in. If you want to start at one minute, then move to three, then five, that's fine. If you don't want to increase the time and simply check in every three minutes or five minutes, that's also fine. The key is to develop a plan that you are comfortable with and to stick with it.

The parent must be out of the room when the child falls asleep. Parents should never shorten the length of check-in time on any given night. If you start the first check at three minutes of crying, do not check in any sooner than three minutes for subsequent checks that night. Use an actual watch or timer to help you adhere to the timing of check-ins. *One minute of a child's crying can feel like an hour.*

If you find that your child is getting more and more upset every time you walk into the room, consider moving to the Cold-Turkey Method as detailed earlier in this chapter.

Just as in solution 1, once the child learns to fall asleep without your intervention, you can slowly move the routine and bedtime earlier by ten or fifteen minutes each night until reaching the desired bedtime.

Solution 3: The Slow-and-Steady Method

Type of caregiver: Can withstand only a small amount of crying.
Typical length of training: Varies, but can take multiple weeks.
Other common names for this method: Camping Out, Fading.

Step 1: Develop a consistent nighttime routine.

Step 2: Identify all sleep onset associations, such as nursing, rocking, singing, and patting. If there is more than one association, the first step is to slowly remove one at a time. On the first night, decide which of the associations you want to remove. So, if you sing to the child, feed the child, and rock the child to sleep each night, eliminate whichever you think will be easiest. Commit yourself to *never* using that association from this time forward to help the child fall asleep. You can certainly perform this activity as part of your routine, but do not use it to help the child fall asleep. The child may have difficulty settling down for the first few nights, but he or she will eventually learn to fall asleep without it. Once your child is falling asleep within fifteen minutes, move onto Step 3.

Step 3: Remove each association one at a time until you are left only holding the child each night. This may take a few weeks. When holding the child is the only association that remains, continue to step 4.

Step 4: After the nightly routine, place child in the crib/bed and sit next to the child. Do not interact with your child in any way, just simply sit there. The child will likely fuss, cry, and try to get your attention. You must ignore this.

Step 5: After a few nights, the child should start falling asleep more quickly. Once he or she is falling asleep within fifteen minutes of being placed in the crib/bed, move your chair two to three feet away from the crib/bed. It is vital that you don't move it closer once you start moving away, no matter how much your child fusses. If your child is mobile and leaves the bed, consistently place him or her back into bed every time he or she attempts to leave—without further interaction.

Step 6: After your child is falling asleep within fifteen minutes each night with the chair two to three feet away, move the chair six to ten feet away and repeat the process. This may take an additional few days to get used to. Caregivers should not leave their chair to console the child or speak to the child. Once your child is adjusted to this, proceed to the next step.

Step 7: Move your chair outside of the room—but still within sight of the child. After a few days, once your child is adjusted to this, proceed to the next step.

Step 8: Move your chair behind the wall, out of view of the child. Once your child is adjusted to this, you're ready for the final step.

Step 9: Put child in the crib/bed each night after the routine, leave, and sleep in your own bed.

If the child wakes up in the middle of the night: Perform the same intervention you did in the beginning of the night. If you are still holding the child in the beginning of the night, you should hold the child. If you are sitting three feet away from the bed, go sit in the chair at the same distance.

It is quite common for children to have multiple associations, such as getting fed, being rocked, and being sung to. Each of these is a separate association for the child. If you take this slow-and-steady approach, you will want to get rid of each association before trying to remove yourself completely. Commit yourself to not reintroducing an association once it is removed. The most difficult association to break typically involves holding the child or sleeping next to the child. I usually wait to eliminate this association until the end. This process can take weeks, but as long as you are committed to always moving in the right direction and not reintroducing associations once removed, this method should eventually succeed.

Remember that you can continue to perform any activity as part of your routine. You don't have to stop engaging in activities that you and your child enjoy. Just avoid the activities at the time your child transitions from awake to asleep.

Solution 4: The No-Crying Method

Type of caregiver: Cannot tolerate any crying.
Typical length of training: Weeks to months.
Other common name for this method: Scheduled Awakenings

Step 1: Determine what time your child typically wakes up at night. If there are multiple awakenings and you are unsure of the timing, create a log that details the times at which your child is waking up each night for the next two weeks.

Step 2: Once you have determined which time/times at night your child tends to wake up, set your alarm to wake up anywhere from fifteen to sixty minutes *prior* to *each* typical awakening. Go into your child's room and wake him or her up at this time (yes, I know this sounds crazy). If your child is waking up only once, you should schedule only one awakening. If your child is waking up three times, you should schedule three awakenings. However, if your child is waking

17

four or more times each night, I would recommend scheduling three awakenings, spaced evenly apart through the night.

Step 3: Once you have awoken the child, do whatever you typically do to get him or her to fall back to sleep, such as rocking, patting, etc.

Step 4: After a few days or weeks, if you consistently wake up the child prior to typical awakenings, he or she will hopefully not wake spontaneously and cry and will only awaken when you wake him or her. Once the child is no longer having spontaneous awakenings at night with crying, start to slowly move back the timing of each of your scheduled awakenings by thirty minutes every three or four days. This will slowly get rid of your scheduled awakenings all together while hopefully still preventing spontaneous awakenings.

Although it is easy to understand how the first three solutions work to teach a child to self-soothe, the reason this last solution works is a bit unclear, since you are still using sleep associations to get the child to fall back asleep. Although it seems to take longer than other methods, it does work. Consider using this method in conjunction with a sleep expert who can help guide you through the process. Be aware that some children will cry for longer than their normal time during a scheduled awakening when this method is first started.

As you can see, each solution described in this chapter has its advantages and disadvantages. Think of these solutions on a spectrum, with lots of nightly crying and fast response on one side, and less nightly crying but a slower response on the other.

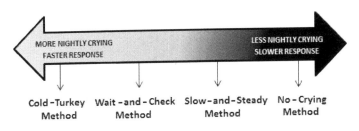

In my practice, if the family doesn't have a preference, I recommend the "Wait-and-Check Method." It seems to provide a nice balance between fast response and a method that parents can stick to. If you pick a solution, try it for a few weeks. If it's not successful try another solution from this chapter.

Here are a few additional tips that you can apply to *all* methods of sleep training:

1. If your neighbors are able to hear your child crying, tell them you are sleep training so that they know to expect it.

2. Buy a good pair of earplugs if you can't stand the sound of an infant crying. But one caretaker should listen for signs of trouble, such as vomiting, fire alarm, etc.

3. Consider starting on a Friday night. You will likely be even more sleep-deprived during sleep training, so plan accordingly. Caregivers should try to get some extra sleep in the days leading up to sleep training. If you are excessively tired, you are more likely to give up.

4. Introduce new sleep associations. Sleep associations don't necessarily have to be a bad thing. A stuffed animal or blanket that is present *only* during sleep and removed from sight during the day can serve as a positive sleep association. Any object that can safely be put into the crib or bed with the child will work.

5. Discuss the plan with all caregivers. Determine each person's role. If all caregivers are not in agreement

with the plan, sleep training is very difficult and can be the source of marital strain.

6. Regardless of which solution you use, even if successful, the problem may arise again later down the road. The key is to go through the same steps once again.

Not Working? Why Not?

If sleep training just isn't working, here are some common reasons:

"I feel guilty."

Caregiver guilt is a common reason why sleep training fails. If a child is crying, the natural response would be to console him or her. But remember, sleep training is not for you. Although you will benefit as well, the main reason to sleep train is for the health and well-being of your child. Not being able to self-soothe and go to sleep independently can be a burden for the child. After all, it means that he or she will have to wake up multiple times each night and cry in order to go back to sleep. This isn't easy on anyone, especially your child. And studies show that sleep is imperative for normal development, learning, and growth. So

21

don't feel guilty. You are *not* doing this *to* your child; you are doing this *for* your child.

"I don't want my child to hate me."

This is a fear for many parents. We worry that the child will feel abandoned and therefore become distant from us. You can rest assured that studies show this is not true. In fact, the exact opposite may be true: *an infant's level of security can actually be better after going through sleep training, not worse.* And remember: children don't start forming long-term memories until around the age of three, so they will not remember anything from this process.

"I don't think I can be so strict."

Many parents think they are just not capable of winning the nighttime battle with their children. Sleep training calls for a level of authority and rigidity that may feel uncomfortable. However, you are capable of making it through this process. Persistence is the key. If your persistence can outlast that of your child, you will successfully sleep train your child.

Not convinced that you can outlast your child's protests? Does your child ride in a car seat? If so, you have already proven that you can win the battle of persistence. Just like sleep training, the process of getting your child into a car seat is not one that most children enjoy. But do you ever allow your child to roam free in the car because they dislike the car seat? Of course not. Why? Because it is for their safety and well-being (and it's the law). So, despite the protests from your child, you get him or her into a car seat every time, and that's because there is just no other choice. Eventually, the child protests less and less since the response from you will always be the same. Treat sleep with the same determination you use for the car seat. Good sleep is also important for a child's health and well-being, just like the car seat.

"My child needs to be fed at night, he is hungry."

Getting rid of nighttime feeds can be tricky. After the age of six months—and often earlier—children can typically go at least six hours without a nighttime feed. However, after the age of six months, children who awaken repeatedly each night for a feed do so because:

   A. They are accustomed to having calories at night and really are hungry, or

B. They have a sleep association with feeding and must be nursed or have a bottle to go back to sleep.

A child can wean off of calories and get rid of the association with feeding at the same time. To wean off of calories, do either of the following:

A. Determine the typical time interval between nighttime feeds. Commit to increasing this time interval by thirty minutes on the first night. So, if your child wakes every two hours to feed, wait two hours and thirty minutes for the next feed. Try everything else to calm the baby if he or she wakes up crying. At this stage, even rocking or patting the child is okay. Every three days, increase the interval by another thirty minutes until you are able to go a full six hours without feeding.

B. Decrease the amount of formula in each feed by one ounce every three days. If nursing, decrease the length of each nursing session by one minute every day. Do anything else to calm your baby to sleep once you reach the limit for that feed.

While weaning calories, also work on extinguishing the association your child may have developed with feeding by keeping the child awake through the feed. If the child is falling asleep, stop feeding and put the child back in bed while he or she is still awake. If the child then begins to cry, implement your chosen sleep-training method.

"My child cries so much she vomits."

This is often the breaking point for many parents. It makes the process of sleep training even more heartrending. I recommend cleaning up the child, changing clothing if necessary, and then resuming the process where you left off. It may sound cruel, but remember that going through sleep training will hopefully prevent many future nights of crying and vomiting. Keep the end goal in mind.

Did your child become a gambler?

The main reason for failure of sleep training is lack of consistency from caregivers. You were able to wait for two hours of crying, but then you had to pick up the child. Or you were persistent for two nights, but on the third, you gave in. Inconsistent response to your child is perhaps the worst thing you can do during sleep training. That is because getting intermittently rewarded makes the child's behavior even harder to change. That is how our brains are wired. For example, when we gamble, we intermittently win. That's what makes gambling so addictive. We keep trying to win, even if we lose multiple times.

If you reward the crying intermittently by feeding or picking up the child, he or she has become a gambler. Your child knows that he or she will win sometimes and get your attention, so the child keeps trying—and trying even harder. This is why consistency is incredibly important. Once you make the decision to sleep train, there should be no turning back. It's an all-or-none commitment.

"Does my child have a medical problem?"

This is a common concern. If the pattern of sleep fits with the presence of a sleep onset association—such as one to five awakenings, typically sixty to ninety minutes apart, with need for caregiver intervention to soothe back to sleep—it's unlikely there is a second problem. If the child is inconsolable at night despite your attempts to soothe, this may indicate pain from teething, GI upset, or other cause of discomfort. Consult your pediatrician if this is the case.

Other Common Questions

1. What should I do about naps?

Children up to the age of four or five years typically take at least one nap. If you are sleep training using methods 1, 2, or 3, I recommend using the same techniques you are implementing at nighttime during the nap as well. However, your child may cry or fuss completely through nap time. If this is the case, I typically recommend that you abort the nap attempt after an hour and resume normal daytime activities. A little bit of sleep deprivation from a skipped nap may help your child fall asleep faster at night. Once sleep training is complete, the child should be able to fall asleep more readily for naps too. I recommend napping in the same location that the child sleeps at night.

2. What should we do if we sleep in the same room?

Similar concepts apply, even if you share the same room. The child has to learn to fall asleep without your intervention for methods 1, 2, and 3. If the child wakes at night, respond according to the method you have chosen. If you are using the "Cold-Turkey Method," do not respond to the crying and simply lie in bed or leave the room. If using the "Wait-

and-Check Method," stay in your bed or leave the room for the appropriate length of time until responding. If taking the "Slow-and-Steady Method," provide the same level of intervention you did when putting the child to sleep at the beginning of the night.

3. Why didn't I have to sleep train my other kids?

All children are different. There are some children who will be great sleepers no matter what the parent does. But for those who are not so lucky, sleep training is important. So don't get discouraged because your first child was different or because your friend has three children who slept through the night without any sleep training. Part of it is simply luck. The other part is prevention. If you start putting your child to bed while he or she is still drowsy during the first few months of life, you are likely to completely avoid the problem.

4. Won't he or she just grow out of it?

Yes, a child who wakes up repeatedly due to sleep onset associations may eventually grow out of the problem. However, the timing can vary greatly. It is not unusual for a five-year-old to still request a nighttime feed or to ask a parent to hold him or her in order to go to sleep. Sleep associations can persist into the teenage years. I do not recommend waiting until the child grows out of the problem since it may take years. Sleep is important for growth and development, particularly during the first few years of life.

5. Can I start sleep training before six months?

For an otherwise healthy child, six months is typically a safe time to start sleep training. It is possible to sleep train children even earlier, and some may respond as early as four months of age. But I tend to wait until six months for children in my practice before attemping these sleep-training methods.

Summary of key points from this chapter:

- Consistency is critical to success!
- Once you start sleep training, don't turn back.
- The process can take several days to weeks. Don't give up on sleep training after just a few nights.
- The most effective and proven sleep-training solutions do involve some crying. But remember that it is for the health and well-being of your child.

- Ignore people who make you feel guilty about a particular sleep-training approach. No matter what you choose to do, you are doing what you feel is best for your child.
- Talk to your doctor before attempting to sleep train if your child has any other medical or psychiatric conditions.

~ Chapter 3 ~
My Young Child Won't Sleep: Ages 1–8 years

There are two main problems that cause difficulties with falling and staying asleep at this age. The first is due to the presence of sleep onset associations, which was extensively covered in Chapter 2. This problem typically involves difficulty staying asleep. It occurs when some sort of caregiver intervention is used to help the child transition to sleep at night (feeding the child, patting the child, holding the child, etc). Then, when the child awakens at night, the same process has to be repeated to get the child to fall asleep. Children with sleep onset associations typically wake up one to five times each night, with at least sixty minutes of sleep in between each awakening. If this sounds like your problem, read Chapter 2. Sleep onset associations can be present at any age.

The second common cause of difficulty with sleeping—particularly difficulty falling asleep—is limit-setting sleep disorder. In this disorder, children make multiple demands at bedtime. "One more story, Daddy"; "I'm thirsty"; "I need another hug from Mom"; or "I need another snack." Do any (or *all!*) of these sound familiar? Children often make such demands to push their limits at night and delay bedtime. If the delay tactics go on long enough, it can cause chronic sleep deprivation and lead to a very cranky child in the morning. Just like it sounds, limit-setting sleep disorder occurs due to lack of appropriate limits imposed by caregivers around bedtime. The child has taken charge at night instead of the parent.

The Solution

There are two strategies for treating limit-setting sleep disorder. Choose your solution based on how quickly you want results and how much tantrum behavior you can tolerate. With each solution, persistence is the key.

Solution 1: The Robotic-Return-to-Bed Method
Type of caregiver: Can withstand severe tantrums.
Typical length of training: Less than 1 week.
Other common name for this method: Silent return to bed.

Step 1: Determine what time the child is currently falling asleep on a typical night. This is the new bedtime. Note: this should not be the time you are placing the child in bed, but the time he or she actually falls asleep. There should be a routine established that starts twenty to thirty minutes prior to this new bedtime and is performed the same way each night. This can include brushing teeth, changing into pajamas, hearing a bedtime story, etc.

Step 2: At the end of the routine, tuck the child into bed and say goodnight.

Step 3: Leave the room. Demands or requests from the child that can delay bedtime should not be fulfilled once the child is in bed.

Step 4: If the child leaves the bedroom, he or she should be taken back into the bedroom, with minimal parental interaction. Parents should not get upset with the child since this response may continue to reinforce the behavior. I recommend repeating one line every time you have to return the child to bed, such as, "I love you, but it's bedtime. I will see you in the morning." The goal is to be as boring as humanly possible—*similar to a robot.*

The child should be repeatedly brought back to the room until he or she eventually gives up and stays in the room. On the first few nights, this may take hours! It is not unusual for a parent to bring a child back to his or her room over forty times! Once the yelling and screaming start, you will likely have to carry the child back to the room. However, once the process is started, the parents should not give in to the child's demands as this may make the behavior harder to change in the future. Do not negotiate with children at night; you will lose!

Alternative Step 4: If the child leaves the room, put up a gate or close the door so that he or she can't leave. If you close the door, only do it after the child attempts to leave and not in the very beginning. Also, only close it for a specified amount of time, such as three to five minutes, and then reopen. If the child attempts to leave, immediately close the door again for the same time period or slightly longer.

Step 5: Provide positive reinforcement the next morning when he or she remains in the room the entire night. Sticker charts work well. Avoid food rewards.

Step 6: Once the child is consistently falling asleep without protest, you can move the routine and bedtime earlier by fifteen minutes each day until reaching your goal bedtime.

If you stick with the above plan and don't give in to the child's demands, eventually the behavior will change. But the process of changing a child's behavior can be difficult because children are incredibly persistent. They always win the nighttime battles since adults don't have the same level of persistence or energy. To treat limit-setting sleep disorder with the "Robotic-Return-to-Bed Method," you have to commit yourself to being even more persistent than your child.

For children older than two, try to explain the process to them prior to starting this method. Get your child's input regarding rewards that can be earned at the end of each week and goals for the week. For example, if the child stays in the room without protest and earns a sticker for three nights this week, he or she earns a small toy. Partnering with your child at this early age can set the foundation for partnership well into the future.

Solution 2: The Happy-Routine Method

Type of caregiver: Cannot withstand tantrums.
Typical length of training: Weeks.
Other common name for this method: Positive routines and faded bedtime with response cost.

Step 1: Determine what time the child is currently falling asleep. This is the new bedtime. Note: this should not be the time you are placing the child in bed, but the time he or she actually falls asleep.

Step 2: Develop a fun nighttime routine with at least five enjoyable and quiet activities. Perform them in the same

35

order every night. At the end of each activity, praise the child and provide positive encouragement, then move to the next activity. The routine should be timed such that it ends at the new bedtime, not sooner.

Step 3: At the end of the routine, tuck the child into bed and tell the child that it is bedtime. If your child attempts to leave, be firm and tell the child that it is bedtime. If he or she becomes very upset and refuses to sleep, remove the child from the bedroom and perform quiet activities until he or she appears sleepy again, and then place the child in bed again. Repeat the process of removing the child from bed each time he or she resists going to bed and then returning when sleepy until the child finally falls asleep. Wake your child at the usual wake time. Don't let your child sleep in. He or she should take the usual length of naps as well—but not longer.

Step 4: On the next night and subsequent nights, repeat the process. Continue to remove him or her from bed if your child gets upset and return to bed once sleepy.

Step 5: Once the child is falling asleep consistently after the nighttime routine without protest, begin to move the routine and bedtime earlier by ten to fifteen minutes every night until you reach your goal bedtime.

If this approach just isn't working for your child, consider trying Solution #1: The Robotic-Return-to-Bed Method.

Remember: regardless of which solution you use, even if the behavior changes, the problem may arise again later down the road. The key is to go through the same steps once again.

It is also important to look for other medical or psychological issues that might interfere with sleep at this age. Here are a few examples:

1. Restless Leg Syndrome: A child who complains of leg pain around the time of bed and appears restless may have restless leg syndrome. Iron deficiency could be the cause, but talk to your pediatrician if this is a concern.

2. Anxiety: Children who complain of "monsters in the closet" typically just need some reassurance. However, some children are truly anxious. Parents can usually determine true anxiety versus delay tactics based on a child's behavior. Truly anxious children may require parental presence and a much slower

transition to independent sleeping. If your child is anxious all the time, talk to your pediatrician.

3. Nightmares: Common among young children, a bad dream is enough to make anyone seek a parent. If a child is truly frightened after a nightmare, it is okay to accompany him or her back into his or her room until the child is calm and relaxed. Reassure your child that it was just a dream. Try to get back to your bedroom while the child is still awake, if possible. If the child is too frightened and insists you stay in the room, it is perfectly okay to stay until the child falls back asleep. Do not get into the habit of allowing the child to sleep in your bed, or you risk making that a long-term habit.

~ Chapter 4 ~

My Older Child Won't Sleep: Ages 8–18 years

The solutions discussed in this chapter apply to children who are making an active effort to fall asleep and are yet unable to sleep at the desired bedtime. Many children at this age have poor sleep hygiene, such as watching TV, playing video games, or frequently using their smartphones at night. If this is the problem, please refer to Chapter 1 to improve sleep hygiene.

For children in this age group who are making an active effort to go to sleep, yet are unable, there are two common causes. The key step to diagnosing the problem is to ask the child one simple question: Do you have a hard time sleeping because you are worried/constantly thinking at night, or is it because you are just not sleepy?

"My Child Constantly Thinks and Worries at Night"

This form of insomnia is called psychophysiological insomnia. It has a big fancy name, but it essentially means that the bed has turned into a place where the child thinks and worries instead of a place where the child sleeps. Adults often have this form of insomnia.

The Solution

The main treatment is reversing this thought process, thereby teaching the child that the bedroom is a place to sleep and relax, not to think and worry. Here are the steps to retraining your child's brain to associate the bedroom with sleep rather than worry.

Step 1: Establish a goal bedtime and wake time. Make sure these times allow the child to get the average amount of sleep needed for someone of his or her age (see chart in Chapter 1).

Step 2: Establish a nighttime routine that starts twenty to thirty minutes prior to bedtime.

Step 3: Adhere to good sleep hygiene (see Chapter 1). All sources of caffeine should be eliminated, including morning caffeine. Bright light sources should be avoided during the nighttime routine, including TVs, laptops, and cell phones.

Step 4: After the nighttime routine, the child should get into bed. If unable to sleep after twenty to thirty minutes, the child should get out of bed and do something that is non-stimulating (such as reading with dim light) until feeling sleepy, then get back into bed. Repeat the process if the child gets back into bed and is still not sleepy after another twenty to thirty minutes. It doesn't have to be exactly twenty to thirty minutes. Don't use a clock, just approximate. The key is avoiding excessive amounts of time in bed while awake.

Step 5: Wake up at the established wake time, regardless of how many hours of sleep were obtained.

Step 6: Avoid frequently checking the clock. Turn the clock around.

Step 7: Make a list during the day. Since bedtime is often the only time of day you get to actually process and think, it naturally becomes the time to worry as well. Every afternoon, have your child make a simple list of things that are on his or her mind. It does not have to be detailed and should take less than five minutes to write. This can include worries, fears, or things on the "to-do" list. Simply writing them down and thinking about them during the day helps prevent children from thinking excessively at night.

Step 8: Avoid naps.

Additional tricks/tips:

1. Take a hot shower prior to bed. The artificial rise, then fall, of body temperature often helps with the transition to sleep.

2. Avoid late evening exercise. This raises the body temperature for long periods, making it harder to fall asleep.

3. Tense each of the muscles in the arms and legs one at a time for a few seconds, followed by relaxing them. Think of the body's tension disappearing as this is done.

4. Instead of thinking about trying to fall asleep, think instead about quietly staying awake. Focusing too much on trying to fall asleep has the opposite effect.

If the above steps do not work, consider seeing a sleep doctor. The next step would be to restrict the number of hours in bed by slowly moving back the bedtime or moving up the wake time. This should be done under the care of a supervising physician.

"My Child Just Doesn't Feel Sleepy at Night"

The most common cause of a young child or adolescent not feeling sleepy at night is called delayed sleep phase syndrome. This sleep disorder falls into a category known as circadian rhythm disorders. What is the circadian rhythm? This is an internal body clock that all living things possess, which regulates a variety of body processes on a roughly twenty-four-hour cycle. One part of the circadian rhythm's job is to make you feel awake at certain times of the day and sleepy at other times. Even if you were put in a cave for multiple weeks without any idea whether it was day or night and no way of keeping track of time, your body would still wake and sleep on a roughly twenty-four-hour cycle. Based on our circadian rhythm, a normal person should feel awake and sleepy in a pattern similar to that shown in Figure 1.

Let's take a closer look at Figure 1. We are all familiar with the 1:00 p.m. dip in our circadian rhythm. We always blame our sleepiness on lunch, but it's mostly due to the internal body clock telling us that we should feel sleepy. At the end of the day, someone with this circadian rhythm would start to feel sleepy around 9:00 p.m. This cycle repeats itself every twenty-four hours.

The problem in delayed sleep phase syndrome is that the internal body clock has shifted so that the body clock is a few hours behind where it should be (it is delayed). For a child whose body clock is delayed three hours, the circadian rhythm would look like Figure 2. The entire curve has shifted to the right. Instead of having the afternoon dip at

43

1:00 p.m., the dip would occur around 4:00 p.m. Instead of getting sleepy at 9:00 p.m., the child gets sleepy around midnight. The typical pattern for someone with delayed sleep phase syndrome is staying up very late each night, sleeping in until late morning or early afternoon on weekends, and struggling to wake up on weekdays in time for school. These children are often very tired and fall asleep during morning classes.

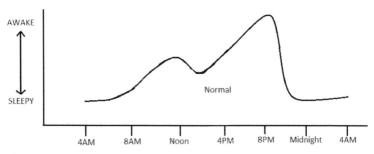

Figure 1: Normal circadian rhythm

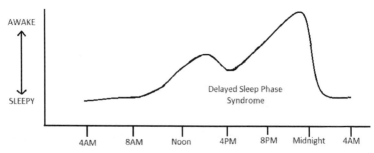

Figure 2: Delayed Sleep Phase Syndrome

Children with delayed sleep phase often skip breakfast because their body isn't ready for food intake in the morning, the same way most of us would feel if woken up at 4:00 a.m. If left to their own devices, these children would prefer to always go to bed late and wake up late. This is a very common disorder among adolescents. If school started at noon instead of 8:00 a.m., this would not be a disorder. But it doesn't.

So what causes the circadian rhythm to shift in young children and adolescents? For some reason, the young brain tends to be very sensitive to the main environmental factor that decides the timing of our circadian rhythm—light. The timing of light exposure sets our circadian rhythm. Getting too much light at the wrong times can cause it to shift. Late-night light exposure causes a delay in the circadian rhythm. And since children are exposed to many sources of bright light at night—such as TVs, smartphones, and computers—their brains are tricked into thinking it is still daytime outside, causing a shift in the circadian rhythm.

The Solution

Step 1: Establish a goal bedtime and wake time. Make sure these times allow the child to get the average amount of sleep needed for someone of his or her age (see chart in Chapter 1).

Step 2: Establish a nighttime routine prior to bed that lasts twenty to thirty minutes.

Step 3: Adhere to good sleep hygiene (see Chapter 1). All sources of caffeine should be eliminated.

Step 4: Avoid exposure to bright light for at least one hour prior to bedtime, including TVs, laptops, and smartphones.

Step 5: On the first night, the child should perform the routine and get into bed fifteen minutes earlier than the current sleep time. This should be fifteen minutes earlier than the time he or she is actually going to sleep each night, not when getting into bed. Each night, move the routine and bedtime earlier by fifteen minutes until reaching the goal bedtime established in Step 1.

Step 6: Upon awakening each morning, try to expose the child to bright lights: open up the blinds, turn on the lights in the room. Flood the eyes with light. This will help move the circadian rhythm in the right direction. The one caveat is for those that have more than a three-hour delay in their body clock.

How do you determine if your child has more than a three-hour delay? Calculate the number of hours between the time your child typically wakes up on the weekend and the time he or she needs to wake up for school. Is this more than three hours? If so, the child has a significant delay. In this case, bright light exposure right upon awakening on school days can have the opposite effect, further delaying the body clock. Try to avoid too much light exposure in the morning until your child is at school. Consider having him or her wear sunglasses while getting ready in the morning. Once he or she is consistently going to bed at the goal bedtime, you can start exposing your child to light right upon awakening in the morning.

Step 7: Consider using melatonin. A small dose of melatonin taken two to six hours prior to the current bedtime can help a child with delayed sleep phase fall asleep earlier. Check with your doctor to make sure it is safe for your child to take melatonin. I only recommend that children use the synthetic (or vegetarian) version of melatonin, and I recommend using the store brand from places such as CVS®, Trader Joe's®, GNC®, or Kerr Drug®. All-natural melatonin typically comes from a gland in the brain of cows. I do not recommend all-natural melatonin to my patients. Small doses of melatonin (0.5mg to 1mg) are usually enough to do the trick.

Step 8: The bedtime and wake time should be kept the same every day—*even on weekends!*

Remember that children with delayed sleep phase syndrome feel similar to those who are jet-lagged. In both situations, the natural body clock is not lined up with the actual clock. Children who sleep until noon on weekends and then get up at 6:00 a.m. on weekdays are trying to shift their circadian rhythm forward by six hours every Monday. That's like flying from Hawaii to New York every week! And unfortunately, the body cannot shift its circadian rhythm that amount in one day. They may finally adjust by Friday, only to repeat the process of delaying their circadian rhythm all over again during the weekend by staying up late and exposing themselves to bright lights at night. Consistent bedtime and wake time throughout the week is critical.

Changing nighttime behaviors can be challenging in this age group. Pre-teens and teenagers are learning to be more independent and will challenge the limits imposed by parents. It is important to partner with your child and come up with a joint plan to tackle the problem. Taking on an adversarial role often leads to undesirable results in this age group.

Conclusion

Sleep is a wonderful thing, but it can be the source of endless frustration. Having an understanding of the common sleep disorders and the tools to address them can be empowering. I hope this book has empowered you. If you are looking for more information on sleep and sleep disorders, follow me on Twitter (@PedsSleepDoc). I wish you and your child a lifetime of a "good night's sleep."

References

Adams L and Rickert V. "Reducing Bedtime Tantrums: Comparison Between Positive Routines and Graduated Extinction." *Pediatrics* 1989:84;756-761.

Ferber, Richard. *Solve Your Child's Sleep Problems.* Simon and Schuster. New York: 2006.

France K. "Behavior Characteristics and Security in Sleep-Disturbed Infants Treated with Extinction." *Journal of Pediatric Psychology* 1992:17;467-475.

Iglowstein I, et al. "Sleep duration from infancy to adolescence: Reference values and generational trends." *Pediatrics* 2003:111;302-307.

Lam P, Hiscock H, Wake M. "Outcomes of Infant Sleep Problems: A Longitudinal Study of Sleep, Behavior, and Maternal Well-Being." *Pediatrics* 2003:111;e203-207.

Mindell, J. and Owens J. *Clinical Guide to Pediatric Sleep: Diagnosis and Management of Sleep Problems.* Lippincott, Williams and Wilkins. Philadelphia: 2003.

Mindell J, et al. "Behavioral Treatment of Bedtime Problems and Night Wakings in Infants and Young Children." *Sleep* 2006:29;1263-1276.

Morgenthaler T, et al. "Practice Parameters for Behavioral Treatment of Bedtime Problems and Night Wakings in Infants and Young Children." *Sleep* 2006: 29;1277-1281.

Pantley, Elizabeth. *The No-Cry Sleep Solution.* McGraw Hill, New York: 2002.

Rickert V and Johnson C. "Reducing Nocturnal Awakening and Crying Episodes in Infants and Young Children: A Comparison Between Scheduled Awakenings and Systematic Ignoring." *Pediatrics* 1988:81;203-212.

Weissbluth, Marc. *Healthy Sleep Habits, Happy Child.* Ballentine, New York: 2003.

West, Kim. *The Sleep Lady®'s Good Night, Sleep Tight: Gentle Proven Solutions to Help Your Child Sleep Well and Wake Up Happy.* Vanguard Press, New York: 2010.

53068775R00039

Made in the USA
San Bernardino, CA
05 September 2017